ARROW FAMILY HANDBOOKS

MAKING ENDS MEET

Arrow Family Handbooks

In any family's life there are bound to be major turning points, choices or moments of decision. Arrow Family Handbooks are designed to explore the alternatives and provide the information and practical advice you need.

Series editor: Mary Gilliatt.

Other titles already published in this series:

Setting Up Home
A basic guide to what you need
Mary Gilliatt

Time Out Together
A practical guide to family leisure out of doors
Caroline Mackinlay

Growing Up
A practical guide to adolescence for parents and children
Catherine Storr

Making Ends Meet

A practical guide to family finance

ELIZABETH GUNDREY

Arrow Books

Arrow Books Limited
3 Fitzroy Square, London W1

An imprint of the Hutchinson Publishing Group

London Melbourne Sydney Auckland
Wellington Johannesburg and agencies
throughout the world

First published by Arrow Books Ltd 1975

Made and printed in Great Britain
by litho by The Anchor Press Ltd
Tiptree, Essex

ISBN 0 09 911290 6

Contents

1. Why Bother About Budgets?

Keeping Accounts the Easy Way. Accounts of Newly-Married Couple. Savings. Accounts of Couple with Child. Bank Statement. How Much is Left Over? How the Bank Can Help – Standing Orders. Budget Schemes. Accounts of Private Spending. What Other People Spend. How Expenditure Rises. Will Your Spending Differ If You Move? Keeping Track of the Big Commitments. About Banks and Giro. How Much do they Charge? National Giro.

What a bore! Keeping accounts is something like slimming or giving up smoking: you really intend to do it – but some other time.

So this necessary chore needs to be kept as simple and painless as possible. For necessary it certainly is at times. Not *every* day, week and year of your life; and not in much detail. But at all turning-points of life it can be extremely illuminating to watch where the money goes: your pattern of spending will suddenly become quite different from what it has been. Especially at times of rising prices it is necessary to keep a watchful eye on things. So budgeting is needed for three reasons: to study how much (if at all!) you are saving; to see precisely where the money is vanishing; and to warn you when you're beginning to head towards debt.

You may be familiar with all your simple expenses as a single person, living in a bed-sit or with the family. But how will that change on marriage? on renting your first flat? on buying a house? when children come? At each turning-point, it can be revealing to keep track of what is being spent each day, over a period of about three months, adding up the totals each week.

Armed with this information, you will then really be able to plan the future to your best advantage. But if you're in the dark about how much you've been spending on what, how can you plan? You may get into debt, or be so pushed for money that you can't afford something you'd dearly like to have, let alone be able to save up for future needs.

KEEPING ACCOUNTS THE EASY WAY

Most household account books are so detailed that they involve a lot of work to fill them in. *Don't buy one.* Instead get a dozen postcards (one for each week, to use up over three months). Put a date at the top of each and some headings down the left side which between them will cover all the kinds of things you spend money on.

ACCOUNTS OF NEWLY-MARRIED COUPLE

Here are seven headings that might suit a young couple, newly married, living in furnished rooms and paying rent weekly. Let us suppose that they are both earning, and they both put the same previously agreed amount into the housekeeping kitty each week (paying for their own clothes, fares, hair-dos, cigarettes, etc. out of their own pockets). By filling in these cards there are less likely to be arguments about money: whoever takes cash out of the box jots the amounts down alongside the appropriate headings. The cards and a pencil are kept in the box with the money.

Week beginning....................

	Amounts spent	Total
Rent		
Gas and electricity		
Food etc.		
Drink		
Entertainment		
Other items		
Savings		
	Grand total	
	Balance left in the cash box	

(The 'etc.' after food refers to things like soap, detergents, and so on.)

After a bit, the weekly cards will begin to show a pattern. Rent is likely to be the same each week, the coins consumed by the gas or electricity meter will be pretty constant too (except when winter brings an increase in heating), and food does not usually vary a lot – except that, these days, its cost goes gently but steadily up. But drink, entertainment and other expenses may well do so and these are the areas where there is much more temptation to be spendthrift, and much more scope for cutting back if economies have to be made somewhere.

On Sunday, everything is added up and the couple can see how they are doing before replenishing the box ready for next week.

SAVINGS

The last heading, savings, is an important one. At the very least, saving up for an annual holiday is a 'must', but this couple might also be wanting to save up for the deposit on a car, or, more vital still, on a house. There is a lot more later in this book about savings and what to do with them. At this stage, the important thing is to be sure of having some money left. The couple could make certain of this, either by deciding on a fixed sum to be saved each week, or by putting aside whatever sum is left when everything else has been paid for that week.

Suppose the week-by-week figures are so tight that there is nothing to go into savings, what then? If no further economies are possible under any other headings, then each partner may need to put a bit more in the kitty every week. And to do that may mean cutting back on some of their personal spending. Where is all his or her money going at present? Once more, some simple accounts could help – showing how much each spends on fares to work and mid-day meals out (probably not much scope for cutting back there); and on clothes, cigarettes, betting, hair-dos and all the rest – maybe one or more of these could stand some pruning.

ACCOUNTS OF COUPLE WITH CHILD

Time passes, and the same couple are now buying a house on a mortgage, and have a child to feed and clothe, and a dog. They need a rather different system of accounts. She no longer earns: out of his pay the husband provides a weekly sum for housekeeping and gives his wife a separate sum for her own personal use. She now does all the shopping for clothes – his, hers and the child's – and so they've decided the money for these should come out of the housekeeping box.

The headings on the weekly cash cards might now look like this:

	Amounts spent	*Total*
Food etc.		
Drink		
Clothes and shoes		
Entertainment		
Repairs, cleaning etc.		
Other items		
Savings		
	Grand total	
	Balance left in the cash box	

What has become of the first two important headings from the 'newly-wed' cards – rent and fuel? Now that they own a house, payments to the Building Society (and also the rates) are made monthly or quarterly by cheque; and the Gas and Electricity Boards are paid the same way. They no longer come out of the housekeeping cash-box.

BANK STATEMENT

To keep track of these cheque payments (and others, like insurance, phone, car licence and tax, HP payments, etc.) is easy because the bank sends in regular statements listing everything paid by cheque. Anyway, with fixed payments (mortgage, rates, insurance, HP, car tax, licences, season ticket, 'save-as-you-earn' and so on) you know in advance what you have to pay and when. After a bit, you're likely to have a pretty good idea what fuel and phone bills average.

HOW MUCH IS LEFT OVER?

By adding all these up (plus any other cheque payments, for furniture or suchlike), and the weekly housekeeping totals, you will soon see what your basic expenses are coming to. Then you can ask yourself: is enough left over for a holiday abroad, redecorating the sitting-room, buying a new fridge, or whatever? And will there then still be a safety-margin for unexpected extras? Or, horrid thought, are you overspending – and if so, what on? Savings at this period of life may well be at a low ebb. It is always wise to save, but the buying of a home and all that goes with it can make this a counsel of perfection for a while.

HOW THE BANK CAN HELP – STANDING ORDERS

Another aid to budgeting, especially if you have a great many regular commitments, is to get the bank to pay them all for you: you simply give them a standing order, saying who is to be paid what and when, and then you don't even have to remember when payments will be due.

BUDGET SCHEMES

If you find many big payments seem to crop up inconveniently at about the same time, the bank may even arrange to add them all up, divide by twelve, and take the money from your account in comfortable monthly instalments throughout the year.

ACCOUNTS OF PRIVATE SPENDING

The simple account-keeping described here does not, of course, cover the husband's (or the wife's) private spending. Sometimes it's worth keeping a separate record of this too. Or a careful motorist may wish to know precisely what it's costing to keep his car on the road: a postcard sticky-taped to the dashboard is useful for noting petrol and other cash expenses as they occur, referring to the bank statements for payments made by cheque in the course of the year.

These are only two examples of how a couple might keep a simple record of their finances, in two quite different ways. There are no fixed rules about how to do it – work out a system to suit your needs. But make it simple – otherwise you're unlikely to keep it up.

And don't rely on memory. Jot down cash expenditure as soon as it's been made: memory is very fallible and you'll quickly find your total doesn't tally with what is in the box.

WHAT OTHER PEOPLE SPEND

It can be interesting to compare your expenditure with other people's. Over a quarter of what the average family spends goes on food. Out of every £10, here's where their money goes. (Figures from Department of Employment for 1973.)

Rent etc.	£1·35
Fuel	55p
Food	£2·44
Drink	47p
Cigarettes etc.	37p
Clothing	88p
Household goods, repairs	79p
Fares, car	£1·36
Services, Entertainment etc.	£1·02
Miscellaneous	50p

As to the vital subject of the food bill, this is where the money goes in most families (figures are per person per week). (Figures from Ministry of Agriculture for 1974.)

Milk (and cream)	5 pints	26p
Cheese	¼ lb	9p
Meat	2¼ lb	£1·02
Fish	5 oz	14p
Eggs	4	12p

Fats	¾ lb	14p
Sugar, jam etc.	¾ lb	10p
Vegetables	8 lb	30p
Fruit	1½ lb	20p
Bread	2 lb	19p
Flour, cakes, biscuits, cereals	1½ lb	29p
Tea, coffee etc.	¼ lb	10p
Miscellaneous		30p

HOW EXPENDITURE RISES

The cost of living goes up every year. Remember this when you try to plan ahead. For example, average spending on food eaten at home rose from £1·80 (per person per week) in 1966 to about £3·25 in 1974 – mainly because prices were going up, but also because more frozen foods were being bought in place of fresh. These are average figures: in well-to-do families, they might be at least 50p more. And naturally adults cost more to feed than children.

WILL YOUR SPENDING DIFFER IF YOU MOVE?

Some parts of the country are dearer to live in than others. London, of course – but in Scotland and Wales too food is 5½ per cent and 2½ per cent dearer than average. In Yorkshire and Humberside, it is 2½ per cent cheaper.

If you moved from a town to a rural area, you might grow some of your own vegetables and thus save money, rent and rates might be lower, car insurance cheaper, and so on. On the other hand, fares to work might cost you more, small local shops are often dearer than city supermarkets, and you might find car usage up because public transport was scanty.

KEEPING TRACK OF THE BIG COMMITMENTS

Fixed sums which have to be paid at regular intervals can

throw your finances out if you've forgotten they are due.
Fill in the figures on a sheet like this (in pencil, so that you can rub them out whenever they change).

	January	*February*	*March*	*April*	*May*	*June*	*July*	*August*	*September*	*October*	*November*	*December*
Rent or mortgage												
Ground rent												
Service charge												
Rates												
Water rate												
Insurances-												
House												
Car												
....												
....												
Life assurance												
HP instalments												
....												
....												
....												
Licences-												
Car												
TV												
....												
Road tax												
Save-as-you-earn												
Subscriptions & fees												
....												
....												
Season ticket												
Other regular payments												

 You may also like to note the months in which other bills will certainly arrive, even though you can't be sure what amounts they will be for: gas, electricity, phone.

ABOUT BANKS AND GIRO

Throughout this book there are references to ways in which a bank can help you if you open an account with one. The most obvious advantages are that a bank is a safe place in which to keep your money, you can pay big bills by cheque, and the statement which the bank gives you shows every item you've paid in and every cheque you have drawn. The statement gives only the number of the cheque and its amount; by referring to your cheque book, or by asking the bank to send you the paid cheques, you can write on the statement the names of the payees – a useful way to keep a record of what you've paid to whom.

HOW MUCH DO THEY CHARGE?

Banks charge you according to the amount of work you require of them – the more cheques you draw, the higher they charge. But if you always keep sufficient money in your account, these charges can be reduced: talk to the bank manager. On the other hand, if you draw out more money than you have put in, you will be charged interest for what is in effect a loan from the bank to tide you over.

Some banks charge more than others, and some may not charge at all, so ask branches of several banks before deciding which one to use. You may find the Co-operative or Trustee Savings Banks (see page 27) charge less than the big national banks, but they may not give you such a wide range of other services. More about that in other chapters.

NATIONAL GIRO

However, for some purposes, the National Giro (a banking system operated by Post Offices) may be the best system of all – and cheapest to use, if your main reason for wanting a bank is merely to pay cheques. Look on some of the bills you receive and you will see that the firms issuing them often print their Giro account number near the address. If you have yourself opened a Giro account at a Post Office, you can get Giro to pay these bills simply by filling in a form, quoting these account numbers, the amounts due, and so on. Giro makes no charge for this service. It will execute standing orders too.

To pay bills which haven't got Giro numbers on them, you can use a Giro cheque book just like a bank cheque book (but you get charged for this). You can draw out up to £30 a time at a Post Office – more if you give a day or two's notice – and for this you will be charged 8p. Post Offices, unlike banks, open on Saturdays. Statements are sent to you free and frequently, complete with names of payees as well as amounts. Loans are obtainable – but you mustn't overdraw.

NOTE

Because of inflation, costs quoted in this book may very well have gone up by the time you read it.

2. Money and Marriage

Keeping one's own Money. Joint Bank Account. Marriage and the Law. Who Earns the Most? Go to Your Bank Manager.

Disputes over money are said to figure more prominently in marriage breakdowns than problems of sex. Although mutual trust cannot be learnt out of books or from systems, at least it is possible to avoid introducing into the marriage partnership, money habits that are bound to cause friction or suspicion.

For either partner to be secretive about income is asking for trouble – although it is known that many men do mislead their wives about their earnings.

KEEPING ONE'S OWN MONEY

But privacy for personal spending (or saving) is another thing: each partner needs to have some pocket money, however small it may be, which is entirely his or her own, to do with as he or she likes and no questions asked. It is humiliating if one partner has to say to the other 'please may I' for every bit of personal spending money.

Decisions about how the household money is to be spent should, however, be arrived at mutually after discussion, though this may be easier said than done if one partner is a miser and the other a spendthrift.

JOINT BANK ACCOUNT

Most modern couples have a joint account at the bank.

 No matter who pays money into it, either can draw this out for any purpose by signing cheques. This is fine so long as each knows what the other is doing, and approves. Otherwise, separate accounts may be better. But whether they have a joint account or not, husband and wife are considered by the law to have a 'common purse' if their general intention has been to share their resources.The husband's pay-packet is regarded as being earned on behalf of both, and to be joint property.

MARRIAGE AND THE LAW

The law has quite a lot to say about husband/wife finances, though for the most part it is only when a marriage breaks down that a couple fall back on Acts of Parliament or decisions of the courts to tell them who is entitled to what. Still, it is worth knowing that, legally, a wife is entitled to keep half of anything she has managed to save out of the housekeeping allowance given to her; that she has certain rights with regard to the house and its contents, even though she may not have made any financial contribution to them; that child allowances are hers not her husband's; that a husband is no longer responsible (as once was the case) for paying bills incurred by his wife without his knowledge; that a gift from one to the other is permanent and cannot be taken back if they later fall out; and that a husband is responsible for maintaining his wife to the same standard of living that he enjoys himself (so long as she is living with him or even thereafter if they separate because of wrongful conduct on the husband's part).

In general, the tendency is for the law increasingly to recognize that a wife contributes a lot in work, even if not in money, to the home, to the family and to her husband's earning capacity; and to see that she is not left unrewarded. Matrimonial law keeps changing, however, so in any dispute a solicitor's advice should be sought early on.

WHO EARNS THE MOST?

It may be that both partners have earnings (or other income) but one has far more than the other. This can cause uncomfortable feelings. Perhaps here more than in any other case the fifty-fifty principle of sharing equally the cost of food and shelter – the basic necessities – is a good one to observe, so that the self-respect of the lower-earning partner shall not be eroded.

GO TO YOUR BANK MANAGER

If you have a good bank manager his advice can be very helpful: he has seen it all a hundred times before, and knows which system of family finance is likely to work best in your particular case. In particular, he is likely to urge any couple to make their wills, no matter how young and fit they are. Even on their honeymoon, one or both might die (in an air crash, for instance). In a simultaneous death such as that, the younger of the two (usually the wife) is deemed to have outlived the other, and then *her* next-of-kin inherits her husband's all: not, perhaps, what he might have chosen!

3. Short-term Saving

Deposit Account. Premium Bonds. Government Savings Schemes. More Flexible Schemes. Investing. Building Societies. Government Stocks.

A cruise or a car, a greenhouse or a greyhound, a baby or a boat, hi-fi or a freezer: all are things which involve saving for, at least for most of us. They can, of course, be bought on credit (well, not the baby perhaps) but as Chapter 6 explains, you still need a deposit. And in any case, buying on credit costs more: sometimes as much as double.

Saving of this sort is called short-term: you're going to take the money out of the piggy-bank or whatever, just as soon as you've got enough.

DEPOSIT ACCOUNT

A lot of people save up by simply banking their money: safer than the pig but no more profitable unless you ask the bank to put it 'on deposit' in a separate account. If you do this the money will earn $7\frac{1}{4}$-$7\frac{1}{2}$ per cent interest (at the time of writing – the rate changes frequently). Not very exciting: you would have to leave £100 untouched for a year for it to turn into £107 – and the £7 interest would incur income tax, reducing it to about £4 in the long run. Not much joy in that if at the end of the year you discovered the price of the object you're saving for has gone up by more than this – all too likely except when there's a price-freeze on.

PREMIUM BONDS

You might just as well take a gamble, buy a Premium

 Savings Bond from your bank or the Post Office and have a 10 000-to-1 chance that your number will come up three months later for the chance of a tax-free prize (£25 to £75 000). Unlike other forms of gambling, you get your money back even if you don't win a prize. Bonds cost £1 each: draws are held weekly and monthly; to get your money back you have to apply in writing and wait a week. But the real solution, of course, is to place your savings where they will attract the maximum amount of interest in an attempt to keep up with price rises.

GOVERNMENT SAVING SCHEMES

The Government is behind a number of other savings schemes open to you: they're mostly intended for people wanting to save up for about four to five years. *You can put your money into whichever you choose by simply walking into a bank or Post Office and asking for what you want.* You can take it out again by applying in writing and waiting a week or two.

Savings Certificates cost £1 and after four years you can cash each one for £1.34 tax-free. (This is equivalent to getting over 11 per cent on an investment where the interest is taxed at 35 per cent.) You can cash the certificates earlier, but you lose the interest.

Saving Bonds cost £5. They earn 9 per cent interest (which has to be declared for income tax). So for every £100 of them which you buy, £4·75 will be sent to you twice a year. But that's not all: if you leave £100 of them untouched for five years, when you cash them you will get £103 free of tax. It's as if you were getting 10·29 per cent on a taxable investment.

'Save-as-you-earn' is a scheme where you guarantee to pay in a fixed amount every month for five years – anything from £4 to £20. You don't get interest but when you withdraw your savings at the end of the five years, you will get a tax-free bonus: linked to the price index. This means your investment should keep pace with rising costs. Further, if you leave your money alone for another two years, you get another bonus, also tax-free. You can withdraw your money before the five years are up but you don't get so much profit. (Regular saving schemes by Building Societies may offer an even better return.)

MORE FLEXIBLE SCHEMES

National Savings Bank, operated through the Post Office, is a good place to put spare money – it will then earn 4 per cent interest at present. You can take out up to £20 whenever you like, or more by making special aplication. (You can even pay bills with NSB warrants, which cost nothing, but to get these you have to write to the Bank's headquarters: more trouble than having a cheque book and account at a commercial bank even if they may charge you.) An added advantage is that the first £40 of interest is tax-free – or £80 if husband and wife have a joint account. This is equivalent to a taxable investment with an interest rate of about 7 per cent.

You can also put your money in an Investment account where anything you put in earns 9 per cent interest at present. But to withdraw money from this one you have to give a month's notice; and all interest is taxable. You are not allowed to have more than £10 000 in an Ordinary account; there's no limit on Investment accounts.

Trustee Savings Banks and the Birmingham Municipal Bank pay 4 per cent, with the same tax exemptions as the NSB and you can also have an Investment account earning up to 9½ per cent, according to the individual bank.

Advantages of TSBs are that you can get a cheque book to use for paying bills (you will be charged 2½p per cheque), that they are more flexible about the amounts you may withdraw on demand, and that they will execute standing orders. Some will even give you loans.

For anyone wanting a safe investment involving no financial wizardry to judge it, the choice is likely to lie among the various Local Authorities, reputable Finance Houses and Building Societies (to distinguish a reputable from a disreputable one, leave the choice to your bank or write for lists of their members to the *Finance Houses Association, 14 Queen Anne's Gate, London SW1* and the *Building Societies Association, 14 Park Street, London W1*. Local Authorities function from Town Halls.

It is better not to invest just a pound or two at a time: a sensible minimum might be several hundreds. Remember that whenever you buy or sell investments you have to pay a small commission to the broker who does the work for you, so making lots of small transactions is an expensive exercise.

The easiest way to set about investing is to ask your bank to do it for you: not only advising you (through its stockbroking department) which organization to invest in, but carrying out the transaction too. Or you can use a stockbroker of your own (addresses of reputable ones are obtainable from the *Stock Exchange, Old Broad Street, London EC2*, or the *Provincial Unit of the Stock Exchange, 3 St Sampsons Square, York*).

Here is what you might get in interest each year.

From a Building Society	7½ per cent tax free (equivalent to 10½ per cent taxable)
From a Local Authority	10½ per cent taxable
From a Finance House	8½-12½ per cent taxable (depending on the amount invested)

BUILDING SOCIETIES

These are a good choice because you can withdraw your

money at short notice (with the others you may have to leave it in for a year at least). You may get a higher rate of interest if you undertake to give advance notice of withdrawal (like six months or a year) and there are some schemes in which Building Societies are linked with life assurance, from which you might get twice as much – your bank or broker can tell you about these. You are not allowed to have more than £10 000 in any one Building Society (or £20 000 in the case of joint husband-and-wife investments).

GOVERNMENT STOCKS

There are also a variety of Government stocks in which you can invest. They have varying rates of interest, and most carry redemption dates (that is to say, the Government will on the date named give you £1 for every £1 share). Because of the rather low interest paid and the limitation of the redemption dates, £1 shares are often sold for far less than this meanwhile and so can sometimes be a good buy if you are prepared to wait till redemption day. What is more, the Post Office sells many of these and charges very little commission. They have lists of what is available.

(Throughout this chapter, calculations relating to tax refer only to income tax paid at 35 per cent.)

4. Thinking Ahead

Owning a Home. Having a Baby. Running a Car. Central Heating.

If you are planning to start a home, have a baby, buy a car or install a central heating system – or any other major enterprise – you will need to have some idea of what the new venture will cost you. There is not only the initial outlay, for which you will need to save up, but also the reorganization of your budget after that to allow for the increased expenditure involved in it. Or, where a washing machine, freezer, caravan or double glazing is concerned, you may be hopeful of cutting costs: see Chapter 5.

The bill for any of these enterprises will obviously differ from one person to another. But here are some checklists to remind you of what has to be budgeted for before you plunge in.

OWNING A HOME

Initial outlay. The finances of buying a house on a mortgage are dealt with in Chapter 7. These pages deal with what is involved in addition to this. For more detailed advice on the subject see *Setting Up Home* by Mary Gilliatt, in this series.

General expenses. Removal from your present address; painting and papering; repairs and alterations; carpets, underfelts (and their laying); other floorings (and their laying); possibly, double glazing, insulation, new wiring; curtains, curtain tracks; heating and lighting fittings (and their installation).

Living rooms. Armchairs, sofas; dining table, chairs, sideboard; bookshelves and cupboards; desk, small tables; radio, TV, aerial; phone (installation); accessories (cushions, pictures, clocks, ornaments, wastepaper bins, etc.).

Kitchen. Cooker (and its installation); refrigerator; washing machine; Dishwasher; vacuum cleaner; kitchen units (and installation); water heater (and installation); ventilator (and installation); kettle, toaster, mixer; table, chairs, stools; saucepans, utensils, etc.; trays; ironing board, iron; brooms, brushes, step-ladder, etc.; china, glass, cutlery; table linen, glass cloths; bread bin, storage jars, garbage bin etc.

Bathroom. Towels, bath mat; medicine cupboard, linen bin, stool; towel rail, mirror; water heater (and installation).

Bedrooms. Beds, mattresses; sheets, blankets, pillows, quilts, bedspreads; wardrobes, dressing tables, bedside tables, chests of drawers; chairs.

Garden. Mower, tools; chairs; possibly, turf and plants.

Upkeep. (Remember that costs of all these are likely to go up every year.) Rent, mortgage payments; rates, water rates, possibly road charges; ground rent, service charge – if leasehold; fuel; phone; cleaning, etc.: not only ordinary house cleaning but window cleaning; dry cleaning of carpets, curtains and upholstery every year or two; chimney sweep; maintenance of gas water heaters and of central heating boiler.

Insurance – of premises and of contents.
Redecoration, inside and out, every few years.
Repairs, breakages, and servicing of electric appliances.
Replacements: carpets are the most expensive item which inevitably wear out. It pays to buy a really good quality so that replacement will not be needed for many years. Electric appliances with motors, and TV, will probably need replacing after ten years or so. Mattresses need renewal when they begin to sag, otherwise backache may result.

HAVING A BABY

Initial outlay. Apart from special maternity garments for mother, even before a baby is born it may cost, at the very least, £50 to provide what it will need:

Nappies and liners – 3 doz (unless you plan to use disposables or a nappy service)	£8
Clothing	£15
Carrycot and bedding	£20
Bath, etc.	£7

Soon after this, a cot and its bedding, high chair, playpen, potty and other things will have to be added, and more clothes – say another £50.

These figures will probably be reduced by gifts, hand-me-downs, home-knitting and so on. And there is a maternity grant (£25 at the time of writing, but it goes up occasionally) obtainable from the local Social Security office, with more for a home confinement.

Upkeep. A baby's needs are obviously not expensive at first, and some welfare foods are free or cheap. The big cost is going to be probably the mother's time if she was earning before but no longer does so. At first, she can get a maternity benefit of £9·80 a week from the local Social Security office, but this stops after eighteen weeks. For all but the first baby, she can obtain a child allowance of £1·50 a week. And parents can claim income tax reliefs.

RUNNING A CAR

Initial outlay. To the purchase price (or deposit if buying on HP) no extras need be budgeted for.

Upkeep. To license and insure the smallest car on the road costs (on average) well over £100 a year. But a much bigger car could cost £250 or more. That's on top of the cost of the car itself, and the loss of interest on the capital you've had to lay out to buy it. Here's how the figures are made up.

Car licence	£40
Insurance	£119 (ignoring no-claims discount)

If you assume a car's life is eight years, then you need to add to these figures something like:

Depreciation	£186
Loss of interest on capital	£112

So the true cost per annum is about £457.

On top of that, there are petrol, oil, tyres, servicing and repairs to be paid for – which will vary according to the number of miles you do. These are likely to come to over 4p a mile. So if you do 10 000 miles in a year, you need to add to the annual bill:

Running costs	£400 (or double that for a big car)

Which gives you a final total of £857 a year (including garage rental). And every year running costs go up.

CENTRAL HEATING

Even before the fuel crisis fuel experts had almost given

up trying to say which system is cheapest: gas, oil, electricity or solid fuel. Not only are prices always altering, but the Government is apt to change its fuel policy overnight – so that what was the most economical system when installed a few years ago, may be proving unpleasantly expensive today. Moreover, fuel prices vary from place to place. The following information, therefore, can do no more than arm you with the right questions to ask when you get some firms to come and quote for installing central heating in your home.

Initial outlay. Electric night storage heaters are cheaper to put in than any system in which you have to add to the cost of radiators (maybe £40–£50 including installation) the cost of boiler-and-pipes. They don't increase the rateable value of the house, and they can go with you when you move. But, they can prove more expensive to run than gas or oil systems. When comparing estimates from different installers, whatever the fuel, be sure to check that they state in writing the following things:

(1) That the system will give you at least 65°F. indoors, even when it's freezing outside.
(2) What the annual fuel consumption will be in order to achieve this result.

A company giving you a low quotation might be planning to give you too few radiators, or too small a boiler, to achieve the degree of comfort you want. On the other hand the more you have, the more expensive the installation – and its future running-costs too.

The National Heating Centre, 26 Store Street, London WC1, has a free leaflet of basic information you may find useful in assessing future fuel consumption.

A final point: is *any* kind of central heating going to be economical? Before rushing in, consider whether you really do want the whole house (or any part of it) kept warm all round the clock. For a couple out all day, this might be a pointless extravagance and a waste of the nation's limited fuel resources. Portable oil, electric and gas fires quickly heat up a room from cold, and are not expensive to buy or install (oil ones are usually cheapest, gas the most expensive).

Upkeep. When you take into account not only the cost per therm (a measurement of heat output) but also the 'standing charge', Gas and Electricity Boards levy, and when you also allow for varying rates of heat-loss up chimneys (except in the case of electricity), then you are likely to find (according to a *Which?* report) that systems using anthracite in gravity-fed boilers, or Housewarm coal in hand-fed Smoke Eater boilers, or oil in pressure-jet boilers, are cheapest to run. Coke, like electricity, is expensive (perhaps twice the price). In between come gas, and oil in vaporizing or wall-flame systems. But these are average findings: in your district things might be different.

Whichever fuel you choose, it's important to get it at the lowest rate you can. Gas Boards offer a choice of tariffs: the subject is complicated so discuss it in detail at the gas showroom (usually, for central heating the 'gold star' tariff is the most economical). Solid fuel can usually be had cheaper if you buy in summer, or by the ton (assuming you can provide adequate storage space). Electricity can be bought more cheaply if you have storage heaters.

Here too a discussion at the electricity showrooms is essential. As to oil, you may get this cheaper if you've a tank that will take a 500-gallon delivery. Both solid fuel and oil prices vary from one supplier to another, so it's worth shopping around.

One more point. A few pounds a year can be saved by cooking on gas rather than electricity (but perhaps at the cost of more frequent repainting of the kitchen: gas isn't so clean); and this saving can be even greater if you get your cooking gas on the lower tariff that goes with central heating by gas. 37

5. Spending to Save

Are you really Saving? A Washing Machine. A Freezer. A Caravan. Double Glazing.

A lot of high-pressure advertising is geared to sell you some costly product on the grounds that it will, in some way, save you money in the long run. True or false?

ARE YOU REALLY SAVING?

You *can* cut laundry costs – but not laundrettes' – by getting a washing machine; a freezer sometimes saves money but not always; obviously a caravan or tent, bought or rented, can provide cheaper holidays than hotels; and some forms of insulation may reduce fuel costs by preventing loss of heat. But each of these also involves extra work as surely as papering your walls yourself, growing your own vegetables, sewing clothes, repairing your car, keeping chickens, making jam and cakes, or shopping around for bargains. Time to someone who might take a paid job is valuable too: convenience is not necessarily a luxury. Every £1 saved is worth far more than £1 earned – if from the latter is deducted income tax which would leave you with only about 60p to spend. On the other hand, every time you spend £1 you are losing the opportunity to invest it and get interest, which could be worth 5p a year (after tax), 50p in ten years and so on. So any saving needs to be greater than that to be worth while.

Here are some facts about what you might hope to save in the long run by making one of the big purchases mentioned above.

A WASHING MACHINE

In March 1975, Consumers Association in their magazine *Which?* compared the cost of washing clothes at home with using a laundrette. Taking the needs of an average family with about 40lb of washing a week, they reckoned that laundrettes cost about the same as an automatic washing machine, plus drier, at home. (Smaller amounts might cost less at a laundrette, large ones more.) Twin-tub machines at home are more economical, however, if you use the same water twice.

Only you, however, can place a value on the sheer convenience of having a washing machine at home, to avoid the time and effort needed to visit a laundrette. Since this comparison was made, all costs have gone up, but the general comparison remains the same.

A FREEZER

There are lots of good reasons for owning a freezer; is economy one of them?

Freezing home produce. If it means you can grow (virtually for nothing) fruit and vegetables and store them cheaply to use later, this is an obvious saving. Fish caught, game shot, chickens or pigs slaughtered, eggs broken out of their shells and packed in cartons: anyone with sources of almost free food such as these can put a freezer to money-saving use, if they are prepared to do the blanching, boning and other preparation needed.

Buying in bulk. Provided the freezer is big, it also enables you to snap up bargains in quantity to keep and use later when other people are having to buy at higher prices: supermarkets' special offers of chickens, for instance, or vegetables at low prices during periods of glut, or purchases at wholesale markets.

You may also buy packeted frozen foods cheaper if you buy them in bulk: look out for cash-and-carry stores.

With meat now so expensive it can be worth buying a big quantity from a butcher willing to give you a lower price for bulk, or from one of the many specialist suppliers of meat for freezers. But beware of those who sell inferior quality or put in too much bone and fat as part of the deal.

Beware also of those bulk buys that merely end in increased consumption: gallon tubs of ice cream are no economy if the result is that twice as much is eaten. The other risk of bulk-buying is a monotonous diet, or the taking-up of valuable space for months on end.

The cost. It costs money to keep food stored in a freezer – far more, in the end, than it cost to buy. For a start, to do any of the money-saving things described above, a big freezer is essential (if you have space for it). The bigger freezers cost less per cu ft to run: a 4 cu ft one, about 7½p a week; a 12 cu ft one, only 15p. A 12 cu ft freezer might cost around £100 to buy, though discounts are common, and would hold some 300 lb of food, an outlay of another £80 or more.

So here is what it would cost you to store food.

£100 for a 12 cu ft freezer with a life of fifteen years (more if you use HP)		£6·66 p.a.
Loss of interest on this £100 and on £80-worth of food (if bought not grown)	After tax	£9
Electricity	At least	£8
Insurance against power-failure spoiling the food; and repairs		£3
		£26·66 p.a.

Is it financially worth it? In the course of a year, a family might eat 900 lb of frozen food. If so, the cost of freezing it would be $2\frac{1}{2}$p per lb (more in a smaller freezer). So any bulk-buys of food *need to show a saving of at least $2\frac{1}{2}$p–3p per lb* if they are to be justified on grounds of economy as opposed to convenience.

But convenience, as already pointed out, can be a money-saver in itself sometimes; and, just as a washing machine may save journeys to a laundrette, so may a freezer save shopping trips.

A CARAVAN

To the cost of buying or hiring a caravan need to be added a number of extras. (An average four-bed caravan will cost over £600 to buy, £15–£20 a week to hire, more in the height of summer.)

The extras. Your car will need a tow-bar and electrical connections to the caravan's lights (at least £30) and possibly wing-mirror extensions; you would be wise to join a caravan club to get many benefits, including cheaper insurance (say £4); the caravan will need equipping with bedding and tableware, unless you borrow from your house; and you may well want to add a refrigerator (£35), shower (£15), separate toilet tent (£14), fire extinguisher, heaters, etc. You will need butane gas cylinders for cooking and heating, and chemical for the toilet.

The outlay will be well justified if the caravan is used by a whole family, and often, the cost of parking on a site is low (around 75p a night) and so the saving on hotel bookings over the years hardly needs to be spelt out.

One advantage of buying as opposed to hiring is that you have extra accommodation for guests; but unless you use the caravan often and not just for one holiday a year it may be better to hire.

DOUBLE GLAZING

Fuel of any kind is expensive, particularly where central

heating is installed. Therefore it can pay to spend money on methods of keeping heat inside the house. Normally, the most dramatic loss is via the roof (because heat rises) and so the few pounds which it costs to lay fibreglass insulation all over the attic floor is money well spent. Nor does it cost much to put insulating strips round badly fitting door and window-frames, and to block up cracks in the floors or disused fireplaces (but don't overdo this, or condensation may result).

Another way of retaining heat is by installing double glazing. The window glass is replaced with a sandwich of two panes and this cuts down the amount of heat that goes out via the glass. It has been claimed that heat-loss can thus be reduced by up to a third, but since it is usually only a small proportion of heat which goes out via the window, such a saving can be shown only in rare cases. After dark, thick curtains might be just as effective.

What it costs. Double glazing can cost hundreds of pounds if the windows are large and there are a lot of them (and if they are not, heat-loss through them is insignificant). It can also double your window-cleaning bill.

This is not to say double glazing isn't worth having: it can add to the comfort of a room by eliminating chilly spots near the windows. But it is significant that no installer will give you any guarantee that it will lower your fuel bills.

NO CREDIT
FOR LOVE
FORLOVE

6. How to Get Credit

Accounts at Shops. Credit Cards. Borrowing from the Bank. Borrowing from Finance Houses. 'Revolving Credit' Schemes. Income Tax Relief. Hire Purchase. Read the HP Document. The Cost. What to do if you Can't Pay. Limit your HP Commitments. Other Kinds of Credit. Check Trading. Borrowing Money to Invest

If you can't wait to get a car, carpet, etc., until you have saved enough money, then you can get it on credit; in other words, obtain the object immediately and pay for it in instalments. This ends by being more expensive, as the person who lends you the money, charges you for this service, so always find out exactly how much he will charge you and see whether you can get cheaper credit elsewhere.

Anyone whose bank will give them a satisfactory reference can obtain a month's credit for buying many goods, and at no extra cost.

ACCOUNTS AT SHOPS, AND CREDIT CARDS

Opening an account at a department store (or at several) is one way: simply tell the store your bank's address and ask them to give you an account.

Having a Barclaycard or Access card (issued by banks) is another: to get one of these, you need only walk into a bank (it need not be your own) and ask for a form to fill in. Provided the answers you give to the questions on it satisfy the bank that you are dependable, you will get a credit card. Then, at any shop (or garage, restaurant, etc.) which displays a notice saying it accepts that particular card, you will be able to buy goods without paying cash: show the shop your card, they will bill the bank concerned, and later (once a month) the bank will bill you for all the purchases you have made with your card. Provided you pay this bill promptly, you will not be charged for this service.

You need to be careful about two things. One is whether shops that give credit accounts, or accept credit cards in lieu of cash, charge more for their goods than other shops do. The other is a matter of your own psychology: are you sure that, if you don't have to produce cash or a cheque immediately, you will not get carried away and order more goods than you can really afford?

If you need credit for longer than a month, or for very big amounts, you will have to obtain it by some other means – and (with the exception of the big mail-order catalogues) pay interest on it.

BORROWING FROM THE BANK

Most people think first of hire purchase, but often this isn't the best way to set about things. If your bank is willing it is better to ask for an overdraft (if your need is temporary) or for a loan (if a longer period is involved or a sum over £100). An 'overdraft' is when (with the bank's permission) you draw cheques for more money than is in your account. A loan is more formal: you make an agreement to pay back a certain sum by a certain date. The interest charged on either of these is much less than you may pay for HP but beware: banks raise and lower their interest rates without notice. A bank's willingness to help in this way depends on three things: their assessment of your financial standing and your ability to repay the money before long, the amount involved, and whether the Government is encouraging or discouraging borrowing at the time when you apply. Some branches, even of the same bank, may be more ready than others to make loans, so *it sometimes pays to move your account.* Interest on an overdraft is at present 13–15 per cent; on a loan it may be either more or less than this.

BORROWING FROM FINANCE HOUSES

You can also borrow money from Finance Houses, but be sure to go only to a reputable one, whose interest rates are reasonable and whose solidity is beyond doubt: you can get a list from the *Finance Houses Association, 14 Queen Anne's Gate, London SW1.* Like a bank, they will check on your financial reliability by asking you questions, and by consulting special credit bureaux whose job it is to keep records of people who have in the past failed to pay bills. Have nothing to do with moneylenders whose interest rates average 40 per cent!

'REVOLVING CREDIT' SCHEMES

It may be that you are going to need credit regularly for a while, for a number of purchases (when furnishing a house, for instance). Some Finance Houses, department stores, etc. operate 'revolving credit' systems – but check how much you will pay for this convenience. Under these schemes, you agree to pay (say) £10 a month, in return for which you are allowed to borrow up to perhaps £360 at any time. You take this out in instalments, as and when needed, to pay bills; and pay interest (which might be 19 per cent or more) only on what you have taken out in excess of your deposits.

INCOME TAX RELIEF

On some types of borrowing you may get a hidden benefit: income tax relief on the interest which you pay. In fact, if your loan is used for the improvement of your house *all* the interest may qualify for tax relief. The Government varies the rules about this from time to time: ask your bank manager for information.

HIRE PURCHASE

Hire purchase is totally different from the methods of borrowing money described above. For a start, you don't own the goods until the last penny has been paid: legally, they are only hired to you and they can, in certain circumstances, be taken back if you fail to keep up your payments (and you can still be sued for what you owe). You cannot sell them, and must not damage them, until they are yours. On the other hand, you are free to stop 'hiring' before all the instalments have been paid if you want to. You are, however, obliged to pay at least half of what all the instalments would have totalled in the end when the goods are taken back.

If the goods prove faulty or wear out prematurely, the person liable is their owner – which may be a Finance House and not the retailer from whom you bought them. But this does not mean you have a right to withhold your HP payments till he puts things right: to do so would merely mean the goods might be taken away from you altogether.

READ THE HP DOCUMENT

Because HP terms are sometimes very unfair, concealing high rates of interest, and doorstep salesmen were notorious for hustling housewives into signing contracts they had not had time to read, the law insists that you shall be given a few days after signing in which to change your mind if you want to. This doesn't apply to HP contracts signed in shops. So be sure to read the document. In a shop, ask for a copy to take home and read at leisure before you sign. It will not only tell you the cash price but also the total your instalments will come to, so that you can see how much extra HP is costing you. It will tell you how many instalments you have to pay, over what period, and how much each will be.

THE COST

HP costs more than you may imagine. The reason is that if a firm charges a low 10 per cent, it goes on charging that right up to the end – even though you have paid off nearly all the price of the goods. This is equivalent to paying 18 per cent on what is actually owed each month. *Beware of shops advertising free credit* – they can only do it by inflating their cash prices. There is no income tax relief on ordinary HP.

WHAT TO DO IF YOU CAN'T PAY

If you get into any difficulties over HP (and a lot of people do – often through taking on too many commitments at once), the Finance House or retailer is likely to be helpful: repossessing goods and suing customers is not good business for them. Your bank manager may help you to sort things out. And HP problems are a field in which Citizens' Advice Bureaux have lots of experience, so a visit to one of them for guidance is well worth while (they make no charge for their help, and have free leaflets on the subject too). Don't go to 'debt adjustment' companies; they are out to profit from your misfortune. And don't just let things drift: these days, records are kept of people who run up debts, and this information may be used against you on some future occasion when you want credit.

LIMIT YOUR HP COMMITMENTS

It is wise to limit HP and other forms of borrowing to well below a quarter of your income, so that you will not feel hard pressed by too many commitments. It is better to put down big HP deposits, so as to have lower or fewer instalments to pay thereafter. And it is well worth shopping around to see who offers the best terms: on domestic appliances, you will probably find the Electricity Board's terms are best (but don't forget to compare the cash prices too).

OTHER KINDS OF CREDIT

Credit sales are different from HP: you own the goods right from the start even though you pay for them in instalments over a long period. Travelling credit-traders calling at the door each week in certain districts often run a kind of revolving credit system; you pay an agreed sum each week, select clothing etc. to have now, and it is paid for over the coming months from your weekly subscription. For this service you are likely to pay interest. You can have more goods even before you've finished paying for the previous lot.

CHECK TRADING

Check trading, common in the North, is yet another kind of credit. For every £1 of checks you want, you may have to pay £1·05 ultimately (in instalments spread over some months). You use the checks to obtain goods at any shops participating in the scheme.

BORROWING MONEY TO INVEST

You can even invest money you haven't got, obtaining it on credit for the purpose. Insurance companies provide the means. For example, if you wanted to invest £1000 but only had £250, an insurance company might put up the other £750. They would want to specify the types of investment to be bought (no high-risk ones), and would require you to take out a life assurance policy of the endowment type (this is explained in Chapter 9), from which the insurance company would benefit too. Of course, you would have to pay premiums for the assurance policy but because you get income tax relief on these, the scheme may provide a cheap way of borrowing money on which you might get a healthy rate of interest.

7. Buying a House

Getting a Mortgage. Additional Costs. Financial Advantages. Mortgages from other Sources.

Now for the most important credit-buying of all – house purchase.

GETTING A MORTGAGE

A mortgage is usually obtained from a Building Society or Local Authority. As with HP you have to provide a deposit (10 per cent or more), show that you are capable of keeping up the instalments, and pay interest on what you are lent – at present about 11 per cent (or, for your first house purchase, 7½ per cent, but you have to go on paying for more years). The Building Society has rights in the property until the last payment has been made (by you, or by anyone to whom, with the society's consent, you sell your interest in the property). After that you own the house and live there free. There are additional complications, of course: the Building Society's surveyor will want to vet the house or flat (and you will have to pay for this to be done) and he may lay down conditions: for instance, insisting that you replace old wiring, or forbidding you to sub-let. The Building Society may think the house is over-priced, and refuse to lend as much as you want.

ADDITIONAL COSTS

In any case, the mortgage will not cover the additional costs associated with house purchase (lawyer's fees, stamp duty etc.) which will come to hundreds of pounds, nor any of the expenses listed on Chapter 4. You can, however, ger a further advance for improving the premises (by central heating, an extra room, etc.); although where some basic necessities (bath, damp-proofing, etc.) are concerned, a loan – or even a grant – from the local Council might be available, if you don't mind the delay involved in getting a decision from them.

FINANCIAL ADVANTAGES

The big value of a mortgage is this. Not only may the value of the house go up every year (much more than any other secure investment would *and* the appreciation in value of one's own home is not usually subject to capital gains tax), but the interest you pay on your mortgage is subject to tax relief. This means that although you may actually pay 11 per cent, the tax benefit in effect reduces this to about 7·4 per cent. (If you don't pay income tax, this doesn't benefit you: so for non-tax-payers there are special 'option' mortgages with a subsidy built in instead.)

You may in fact do very much better than this. There are, for example, ways of linking mortgages with life assurance which may give you a much better deal. All the time, new schemes are made available: this is where a good bank manager is really worth having, for he knows or can find out the best method for your particular circumstances. For instance, you might want a mortgage with low payments now and higher ones later, while another buyer might prefer the reverse of this.

MORTGAGES FROM OTHER SOURCES

Most Building Societies charge a lower rate of interest than most Local Authorities, but the latter are sometimes willing to lend on property which Building Societies don't favour (older houses, for example).

Building Societies themselves vary in what types of property (and types of householder) they favour most. Their attitudes to working women vary, too. They also differ in reliability, so to avoid picking a lemon obtain a list of reputable ones from the *Building Societies Association, 14 Park Street, London W1.* Or take your bank manager's advice.

Other organizations that provide mortgages include insurance companies (they tend to be interested only in bigger houses and professional people), banks (only over a shortish period), employers (if they can induce you not to change jobs), or sometimes friends, solicitors, or even the vendor of the house. But check their terms even more carefully than usual.

8. Saving for the Future

Long-term Investment. Where to get Advice.
What is the Risk? Unit Trusts.

Although we live in a Welfare State, anyone who relies entirely on its handouts for the harder times of life is in for a meagre time. Things like unemployment or sickness benefits, family allowances or retirement pensions, are useful supplements to one's own resources – but are not meant to take the place of personal savings. It is no good waiting until need arises: the time to think about it, and provide against it later, is when all is still going well.

There is an extra liability which many families encounter now that people live longer: helping to house or otherwise provide for ageing parents.

LONG-TERM INVESTMENT

Since its purpose is to provide money maybe ten to twenty years hence, quite a different choice of investments from those described in Chapter 3 may be appropriate, since you will not be intending to fish your money out again for a long time. A broker will advise you that certain investments offer you a particularly big return if they are left untouched for many years, and these are the ones to select now. If you are prepared to forego a high rate of interest here and now, you can get a better reward when ultimately you sell and find that every £1 of capital you invested brings (possibly) several pounds when sold. Even though the Government takes some of your profit (by levying a capital gains tax), you will still be better off than if you had chosen investments giving you a higher interest now (subject to income tax) but selling later for little more than their purchase price.

WHERE TO GET ADVICE

Everything depends on choosing your investments wisely. And unless you intend to become quite expert yourself, this is where you need a stockbroker, or the investment department of your bank, to help you do your choosing; though the more knowledgeable you become the better you will be able to comment on their recommendations, after all, no one is quite so keenly interested in seeing you prosper as you are yourself! Addresses of reputable stockbrokers are obtainable from the *London Stock Exchange, Old Broad Street, London EC2,* or the *Provincial Unit of the Stock Exchange, 3 St Sampsons Square, York.*

Reading the articles on investments in newspapers (the *Financial Times* or the *Investors Chronicle,* if you are really keen) is a good beginning. There are plenty of books on the subject of investment for beginners; one of the best is *The Save-and-Prosper Book of Money* (Collins, £1·75) and, unlike many, it is brought up-to-date annually. Consumers' Association, who publish *Which?* also publish *Money Which?* which makes impartial comparisons of certain types of investment.

WHAT IS THE RISK?

Apart from very safe things like those described in Chapter 3 all investments carry some risk: if the business you invest in doesn't go well, you get less benefit; if it does very well, you get more. Obviously, you want to avoid enterprises that look highly profitable but are also highly risky. But when investing in things like ICI or Marks & Spencer, 'risk' is minimal. Provided always that you can leave your money in for many years if need be – even ICI has bad periods at times. By putting money into a variety of companies, you can expect to gain on the swings anything you may unfortunately lose on the roundabouts. And you can eliminate much of the risk by sticking to debenture or preference shares, which bring you a guaranteed rate of interest no matter what happens (unless the company collapses).

UNIT TRUSTS

Risk-spreading is where the Unit Trusts and Investment Trust Companies come in. Each Trust invests its funds in a whole number of carefully chosen companies. By buying units (shares) in the trust, you get an indirect share in all those companies – chosen by experts in investment. Even if some don't do so well, you can hope all the rest in the package will make up for this. There are now all sorts of elaborate schemes associated with Unit Trusts: for instance, units combined with life assurance (bringing income tax concessions, as described in Chapter 9), and for buying on a regular investment basis.

Because Unit Trusts and Investment Trust Companies are a particularly safe investment for beginners, it is a good idea to study them in particular and you can get from the *Wider Share Ownership Council, c/o Charles Baker Ltd., 30 Farringdon Street, London EC4* a free booklet called '7 Ways to Invest in Shares'.

Of course, not all investors will be looking for a long-term increase in the value of their investments. Later in life, high interest immediately may be what's needed. Then will be the time to switch from one type of investment to something different. All this is far removed from 'speculation', which is what some people wrongly imagine investment is all about: perpetually buying and selling to make a fast buck. Most investment is not at all like that, and speculating is a professional game.

9. Life Assurance

How It Works. Advantages as a Method of Saving. Disadvantages as a Method of Saving. Where to get Advice.

HOW IT WORKS

Life assurance means what it says: it assures you of certain benefits in connection with your life.

Any responsible husband must (because men's lives usually end several years earlier than women's) give thought to his wife's position at his death. He would be relieved to know she would then get a lump sum, or an annuity, to supplement her small widow's pension when he can no longer provide for her – no matter whether he dies soon or not for a long time to come.

He may be particularly worried about her situation and the children's, if he dies prematurely, leaving her with a mortgage still to be paid off and children to keep. And even if he were to live to a ripe old age, he still needs to think about the requirements of both of them when he ceases earning – few pension schemes provide really adequately for old age.

To provide for such eventualities, you can make regular payments (premiums) throughout your earning years in order to buy life assurance for any or all of the following:

A lump sum – or annuity – paid to your widow (or other heirs) when you die: this is called whole-life assurance.

The same, but only if you die before a specified date – i.e. prematurely: this is term assurance.

Term assurance *plus* a guarantee that the sum will be paid on the specified date if you are still alive then; this is endowment assurance.

Life assurance companies can provide you with these benefits largely because meantime they have your premiums to invest profitably. By paying a bit more, you can have a 'with-profits' policy – which means you get an additional bonus related to whatever profit the company has succeeded in making.

ADVANTAGES AS A METHOD OF SAVING

As a method of saving for the future, life assurance is better than many investments because it is safe, it offers you a good return on your money (though naturally not as good as some riskier investments may be) but above all because you get income tax relief in respect of the premiums you pay, which (for most taxpayers) is equivalent to getting back over 15 per cent of what you have paid out.

DISADVANTAGES AS A METHOD OF SAVING

Its main disadvantage is that you lose much of the potential return on your money if for some reason you suddenly need capital and have to cash the policy. However, this is usually avoidable because assurance companies, banks and Finance Houses are as a rule happy to lend money (at the usual rate of interest) to anyone with a life assurance policy to offer as security against the loan. Nevertheless, it is wise to have only some of your savings in life assurance, with the rest invested (see Chapter 8) and therefore more easily accessible if need arises.

WHERE TO GET ADVICE

There are lots of more elaborate systems of life assurance, catering for different individual circumstances. The best person to consult in the first place is your bank manager, who will be able to find out for you which life assurance company and which type of policy would give you the best deal. Or you can go to an insurance broker (addresses of reputable ones are obtainable from the *Corporation of Insurance Brokers, 15 St Helens Place, London EC3*). Brokers get commission from the life assurance companies, so they will not recommend two companies which pay no commission but in fact offer very good policies, these are *London Life Association, 81 King William Street, London EC4*, and *Equitable Life Assurance Society, 4 Coleman Street, London EC2*, so write to these two yourself for particulars of what they offer.

You can obtain a free booklet on all the different aspects of life assurance by writing to the *Life Offices Association, Aldermary House, Queen Street, London EC4*. This is an organization representing most of the assurance companies.

10. Insurance

How Insurance Works. National Insurance. Insurance against Permanent Illness. Help from Friendly Societies. Private Medical Treatment. Medical Expenses Abroad. Insuring your Car. Insuring your Home. Insuring the Contents of your Home. Injuries to Yourself. Who can Advise You?

If you get through life without a single fire, theft, car accident, major illness, unemployment, injury or claim for injuring someone else, you will be quite exceptional.

Nothing, of course, can take away the suffering or loss that such things bring. But at least their cost can be taken right off your shoulders by insurance.

HOW INSURANCE WORKS

The principle behind insurance is simple. If 100 people pay a very small premium to be insured, maybe only one of them will ever need to make a claim; his tiny contribution entitles him to benefit from the total paid in by all 100 contributors (and any interest earned by that money). The other ninety-nine may never need to make a claim; but they have the peace of mind that comes from knowing they can do so if ever misfortune should strike.

You can insure against pretty well any eventuality – from rain spoiling your holiday to giving birth to twins. But the greater the risk, the higher the premium: insuring against rain in Ireland would cost more than insuring against it in Greece.

NATIONAL INSURANCE

You are to some extent insured against unemployment by the compulsory contributions taken from you (and your employer) by the Government – the stamps on your National Insurance card. National Insurance also entitles you to benefit if you have an accident at work, get a disease caused by your work, are made redundant or are too ill to work. The State also provides a death grant to cover funeral expenses, and makes weekly payments to widows for six months. But none of these benefits is on a very generous scale, so private insurance to supplement them can be money well spent.

INSURANCE AGAINST PERMANENT ILLNESS

In particular, it may be well worth insuring against any more-or-less permanent illness or injury that might reduce earning capacity. This is different from, and better than, some private insurance schemes that offer to pay you while you are in hospital: hospital stays are usually brief – it's long disablement thereafter which can cause real financial hardship. Details from the *Permanent Insurance Company, 7 Chandos Street, London W1.*

HELP FROM FRIENDLY SOCIETIES

There are also hundreds of Friendly Societies and sick clubs which provide limited (sometimes very small) sums for periods of illness: the *Registry of Friendly Societies, 17 North Audley Street, London W1,* can give you information.

PRIVATE MEDICAL TREATMENT

If you want to have a private room when you go into hospital, which is very expensive, you can insure for this, and other private medical treatment including home nursing, through organizations like the *British United Provident Association, Provident House, Essex Street, London WC2,* or *Private Patients Plan, Eynsham House, Tunbridge Wells, Kent.* Less expensive than private rooms are shared ones, but only some hospitals provide these 'amenity beds'.

To cover the cost of the extras that so often go with illness but which are not wholly covered by the Health Service (convalescence, home help, physiotherapy, hearing aids, as well as extra sickness benefit) there are other insurance schemes available. Details of them are obtainable from the *British Hospital Contributory Schemes Association, 87 Lord Street, Liverpool 2.*

MEDICAL EXPENSES ABROAD

Where medical expenses abroad are concerned, in the many countries where you cannot avail yourself of a free health service, it is necessary to insure separately. Most travel agents can fix this for you when you book a holiday, with insurance that also covers things like lost baggage or having to cancel your holiday because of illness, and compensation for injury.

INSURING YOUR CAR

One of today's major hazards is motor accidents. The law demands that every motorist is insured against injury done to others, so that his victims can get some compensation. But most car-owners are wise enough to take out fuller insurance. The most thorough coverage is given by 'comprehensive' insurance, which embraces fire, theft and damage (to your car, other cars, or other property), as well as some help if you yourself are injured – and it even caters for the situation when someone else is driving your car, or you are driving someone else's. Extra insurance is needed for such things if you go abroad. Consult your car insurance firm who will issue you with an internationally-accepted insurance form (a green card).

INSURING YOUR HOME

Where your home is concerned, two kinds of insurance are desirable: for the building and the contents. If you don't own the house, then the landlord should insure it; tenants, however, have a right to make claims under a policy taken out by the landlord. For most people, fire is the hazard likely to cause the biggest loss – so insurance should be adequate to pay for rebuilding the structure (which, every year, costs more) but need not cover the value of the site, of course. This type of insurance normally covers all sorts of other hazards – such as damage by leaking pipes (water or oil), lightning, floods, cars or planes crashing into it, broken sinks and windows.

INSURING THE CONTENTS OF YOUR HOME

House insurance costs little; insuring the contents is a bit more expensive, largely because theft is such a distinct possibility these days. Many people under-insure, and this (as with other insurances) means the company may reject any claim you make, or not meet it in full. It is important therefore to list all the contents (the checklist on page 32 may help you – but don't forget to include clothes, books, jewellery, records, etc., as well) and to put down what it might cost to replace each of them at today's prices. Remember to keep your list up-to-date. If, however, a carpet, cooker etc. is not new, reduce this figure accordingly. At the same time, write down the serial number of electric appliances, typewriters, etc., to enable the police to recover your property if it is stolen.

Insurance of the contents of a house often covers their loss even when they have been taken out of the house (for instance, if they are in your workplace or if you have taken them on holiday). Read your policy carefully so that you know what it covers.

INJURIES TO YOURSELF

A house contents policy also gives some cover for your

liability for injuries to people visiting your home, but if you want really full coverage for injuring people, that costs more. As to injury you might sustain yourself, you can insure against this with a special 'personal accident' policy: but the more hazardous your work or pastimes, the higher the premium. If you are injured by a criminal or by a car and cannot get compensation from the man responsible, you may be able to get it from the *Criminal Injuries Compensation Board, Russell Square House, London WC1,* or The *Motor Insurers Bureau, Aldermary House, Queen Street, London EC4* without having had to take out insurance for the purpose.

WHO CAN ADVISE YOU?

Having decided what insurances you think you need, discuss the subject with your bank manager, or with an insurance broker. Addresses of reputable ones can be had from the *Corporation of Insurance Brokers, 15 St Helens Place, London EC3.* Both these know how the different insurance companies compare with one another. The cheapest may not be the best, it may be one that is about to go broke, or it may be mean and slow when it comes to settling claims. Some companies discriminate more than others against certain types of people whom they consider a bad risk. The bank's insurance department, or a broker, should know which companies, and which types of policy, best cater for your particular needs.

Citizens' Advice Bureaux have cheap booklets on the subject. Consumers Association have a £1 book, *Claiming on Home, Car and Holiday Insurance* (their address is *14 Buckingham Street, London WC2*), and you can get free leaflets from the *British Insurance Association, Aldermary House, Queen Street, London EC4.*

11. Your Rights

The National Insurance Scheme. The National Health Service. Finding out what is Available. Help with Children. Help for Handicapped Children. One-Parent Families. Other Allowances. Help for the Elderly. Housing for the Elderly. Legal Expenses. How to Make the State Pay Up. Getting Help from your MP.

Nearly everyone pays their bit towards the Welfare State, mainly through taxes and by contributing to National Insurance. In return, everyone is entitled to certain benefits: pensions; maternity and family allowances and the financial help given in times of trouble, unemployment, illness, some injuries, death and so on. For those who are really hard up, there are supplementary benefits to help make ends meet. Leaflets about all these, and application forms, are obtainable from local Social Security offices, or, in the case of things to do with unemployment, local Employment Exchanges.

THE NATIONAL INSURANCE SCHEME

Most of these benefits, except the last, are available only to people who have contributed to the National Insurance scheme (through weekly stamps on a card). Wives are, for the most part, covered by their husbands' contributions. As a married woman it is worth making quite sure you know what your husband is paying in terms of stamps for you and what this entitles you to. If he dies suddenly or you divorce, you might find yourself not eligible for things that you thought were yours of right. It really is worthwhile to know before it is too late so that you can decide whether you want to pay for your stamps independently.

Self-employed people can't get unemployment benefit; while non-working people can get neither unemployment nor sickness benefit. They therefore pay lower contributions than the joint employee/employer contributions made on behalf of most workers.

THE NATIONAL HEALTH SERVICE

It is in part these National Insurance contributions which help to finance the Health Service, too – though everyone is entitled to use this, whether they make contributions or not. The Health Service provides you not only with the services of doctors and hospitals, free, but also a range of other assistance, either free or at a specially low price. The following is a list of what some, but not necessarily all, areas offer (though, in many instances, only for certain categories of need): maternity clinic services (including welfare foods), health visitors at home, contraception and abortion, home help and home nursing, special nursing or other equipment, dentistry, chiropody, medicines etc. on prescription, vaccination, fares for visiting a distant hospital, convalescent homes, recuperative holidays, free laundering of sheets etc., physiotherapy (sometimes at home), care for children whose mother is in hospital, night attendants, school health and dental service, child guidance (psychological), home alterations for handicapped people, spectacles, hearing aids, dentures, and also special clinics and a wide range of services for the elderly.

You can obtain homoeopathic treatment free under the Health Service but not other unorthodox treatment like acupuncture, osteopathy and so on.

FINDING OUT WHAT IS AVAILABLE

Whenever you have a need of this kind, the best person

to ask about what is available is probably your doctor; or else approach the Social Services, or Welfare department of the local Council. Often, what is available officially is supplemented by voluntary organizations, so you could also try your local Women's Royal Voluntary Services, Red Cross and local Council of Social Services. *A Consumer's Guide to the British Social Services* (Penguin 50p), is a useful book to keep on your shelves. It covers all these services and many others too.

HELP WITH CHILDREN

If you have children, it is worth checking whether you are getting all that you are entitled to: the main source of information and help is likely to be the local Education Authority. For example, your children might be entitled to free transport to school (if the school is some distance away), reduced fares on other journeys, reduced charges for school dinners (if the family is large and hard up) sometimes even continuing through the school holidays, grants for school clothes, free loan of sports clothes and gear or other special things, allowances for clothes and other expenses, when children continue to be educated beyond the compulsory age, special schooling while in hospital, boarding-school fees in cases where boarding is for some reason desirable and even fees at private day-schools in certain circumstances. It can be worth consulting the *Advisory Centre for Education, 32 Trumpington Street, Cambridge*. A small fee for advice has to be paid.

HELP FOR HANDICAPPED CHILDREN

In addition, there is an even wider range of assistance to be had for handicapped or delicate children – not only official but from organizations like the Invalid Children's Aid Association, the Shaftesbury Society, the National Society for Mentally Handicapped Children and many others. If you have a special problem of this or any other kind, your local Citizens' Advice Bureau or Council of Social Service can tell you of organizations that help, and will recommend useful books or leaflets.

ONE-PARENT FAMILIES

One-parent families are up against particular problems, not least financial ones. In recent years there have sprung up several organizations addressed to their special needs. *The National Council for One-Parent Families* (motherless as well as fatherless) is at *255 Kentish Town Road, London NW5*: it developed out of a council for unmarried mothers but widened its coverage a few years ago. For the widowed there are the *Cruse Clubs, 126 Sheen Road, Richmond, Surrey*, while for the divorced there is the *National Council for the Divorced and Separated, 13 High Street, Little Shelford, Cambridgeshire*. Then there is also the *National Council for the Single Woman and her Dependents, 166 Victoria Street, London SW1*. Finally, for men coping with a motherless family, *Families Need Fathers* is run by K. Parkin, *25 Combe Park Road, Bath*; while its all-women counterpart is *Mothers in Action, 9 Poland Street, London W1*. All these give advice, and have a variety of pamphlets or other publications.

OTHER ALLOWANCES

If you are caring for someone else's children, even those related to you or of whom you are the guardian, you can obtain a fostering allowance. A divorced mother is entitled to a special allowance if the father dies.

HELP FOR THE ELDERLY

Special concessions for the elderly are numerous but tend to vary from place to place. They can include free recreational clubs, meals (at a club or at home), financial assistance over and above any pension – either from the

Social Security office or from one of the many voluntary organizations which have funds for those in need (details of these can be had from the *Family Welfare Association, 501-505 Kingsland Road, Dalston, London E8*), rate rebates, rent subsidies, cheap or free tickets for all sorts of things (buses, laundrettes, haircuts, dry cleaning etc.). Most towns have an Old People's Welfare Committee from whom one can get information. Otherwise ask the local Citizens' Advice Bureau, Women's Royal Voluntary Service or Red Cross. Addresses can be found in the telephone directory, or ask at your local library.

For those who are not very fit, the Local Health Authority may run day-hospitals, clinics and centres which not only provide things like physiotherapy or chiropody but meals, transport and recreation.

HOUSING FOR THE ELDERLY

Special subsidized housing designed for the elderly (often with a warden to keep an eye on them) may be provided by the local Council, or by one of the many housing societies set up for this purpose. Details of the latter can be had from the *National Federation of Housing Societies, 86 Strand, London WC2* and the *National Association of Almshouses, Billingbear Lodge, Wokingham, Berkshire.* The local Council has powers to make alterations to ordinary homes to make them more convenient for elderly people who are getting infirm – usually at low cost, sometimes free. If free places are not available in Council-run homes for old people (many of which are gruesome, yet applications outnumber places), then grants may be obtainable towards the high fees charged by privately run homes. Details about the latter can be had from the *Family Welfare Association, 501-505 Kingsland Road, Dalston, London E8,* the *Elderly Invalids' Fund, 10 Fleet Street, London EC4* and the *Distressed Gentlefolks Aid Association, Vicarage Gate House, London W8.* Some local Councils are good at boarding-out elderly people, in special lodgings; or, to give relief to relatives looking after an old person at home, they provide free or low-cost holidays, sitters-in (day or night), domestic help, laundry services, and outings.

For elderly people alone in their own homes there may be available (free or cheaply) television or radio. Or helpers will come round to do home repairs, redecorating or gardening, or visitors can come to read aloud, write letters or go shopping; while a mobile library, chiropody, nursing, etc. can all be provided at home. Even dentists and opticians may call, free, if a doctor certifies the need for this.

Some local Councils also provide telephones (under an agreement with the GPO) for the registered disabled or elderly people alone in their homes, the Council paying installation charges and quarterly rentals.

LEGAL EXPENSES

To get your rights, it is sometimes desirable to consult a solicitor, or even to retain a barrister to fight your case in court (although in simpler cases you can go to court without a barrister if you wish). Both solicitors and barristers are expensive to hire, but there is now a legal advice and aid system under which their services can be had without charge, unless your means exceed a certain amount (which was recently raised, and may go up again).

There is no formality beyond filling in a form at your solicitor's office (choose one who belongs to the scheme) until you want to move on to court proceedings, and then there will be some searching enquiries into your means. To find a solicitor ask at a Citizens' Advice Bureau or look in the Yellow Pages of the telephone directory.

HOW TO MAKE THE STATE PAY UP

You may feel you are entitled to some benefit from the

State which in fact is being withheld. You can always appeal against the decision of an official; there is a network of tribunals to which you can take your case. They cover pretty well every kind of dispute you may have with officialdom, from compensation for an accident at work, to disagreement over how much income tax you owe. Citizens' Advice Bureaux can tell you how to get started on this course.

GETTING HELP FROM YOUR MP

Another way to press your case may be to write or speak to your MP (it doesn't matter whether you voted for or against him at the election). Get his name and address from your local library. He is in a position to take up your problem with the government department concerned, or he may get the Parliamentary Commissioner ('ombudsman') to investigate the complaint – this depends what it is about. Local borough or county councillors are supposed to act for you if the matter concerns a council department.

There are in addition various organizations which will sometimes fight legal battles on behalf of their members – for instance, the AA and RAC, British Legion, trade unions etc., particularly if they feel the case has a bearing on the rights of their members as a whole. For disagreements over bills see Chapter 12.

12. Getting Your Money's Worth

What to do First. Are you Protected by the Law? Is this your Problem?

From time to time, everyone makes a bad buy, or pays somebody to perform a service which is badly done. Or you may be asked to pay something which you don't feel you really owe or you may be overcharged; or enter into a commitment which turns out not to be what you supposed. Sometimes, you suffer actual harm as the result of a purchase; faulty brakes on a new car could cause immense damage and injury, for example.

WHAT TO DO FIRST

In the majority of cases, taking your complaint to the person responsible is enough to secure satisfaction: a clear (and unimpassioned) account of what went wrong is the first step to take. But when you are up against someone who refuses to accept liability, what then?

ARE YOU PROTECTED BY THE LAW?

In many cases, there will exist a law that protects you, and possibly an organization that will fight on your behalf. To find out whether this is so, a good move is to ask the nearest Citizens' Advice Bureau. If the matter is both complex and serious, a solicitor may be needed (see Chapter 11 on how to get his services free under the legal advice system). In some neighbourhoods, there are now law centres where solicitors can be approached in a very informal way for advice, ask your local library for the address. *The British Standards Institution, 2 Park Street, London W1,* has a free leaflet, 'How to Complain'.

IS THIS YOUR PROBLEM?

Here is a list of some common areas in which you might run into disputes of this kind. (Note that even when you've not paid directly but only through taxes you may still be entitled to redress for bad service – see under Medical.)

Cars and garage services. The AA, *Fanum House, Basingstoke, Hampshire,* and RAC, *89 Pall Mall, London SW1,* may help you if you are a member; the *Motor Agents Association, 201 Great Portland Street, London W1,* if the dealer or garage concerned is a member. See also Goods.

Coal, coke etc. See Goods.

Food etc. Underweight or misdescribed: see Goods. Stale or polluted: go to the Public Health Department at the Town Hall. (See also Prices.)

Gas and electricity bills. Every Gas or Electricity Board has a Consumers' Consultative Committee attached to it (address obtainable from the Board), one of whose tasks is to investigate disputes between consumers and the Board. Accounts departments make mistakes more often than the meters do, but you can ask for the meter to be checked (there is a charge for this if it turns out that there is nothing wrong with it).

Goods: defective, misdescribed or underweight. It is now quick and easy to take small claims to county courts where a Registrar (a kind of judge) will deal with them without the usual procedures of a law court. For information, ask at any court. Misdescriptions (e.g. describing a hotel as 'by the sea' when it's miles away, or a second-hand car as 'in perfect order' when it is rusty underneath) might be prosecuted by your local Fair Trading Officer and you might then be given compensation: enquire at the Town Hall. The same applies to being given short weight. If you feel these procedures are too strong, you might get your local Consumer Advice Centre or Consumer Group (address obtainable from your Citizens' Advice Bureau or local library) to intercede on your behalf or (particularly where clothes and furnishings are concerned) the *Retail Trading Standards Association, 356 Oxford Street, London W1.* See also Prices.

Guarantees. The fact that a manufacturer has issued a guarantee does not exempt the retailer from liability. Under the Sale of Goods Act, it is up to the retailer to see that the product is all it should be – *even after the guarantee period has run out.*

Hire purchase. See page 48.

Holidays and travel. The same general principles apply as for all other goods and services. In addition, the rail and air transport services have consumer committees like the ones described under Gas. (The rail and air services can supply their addresses.) *The Association of British Travel Agents, 53 Newman Street, London W1* will investigate if your travel agent is an ABTA member.

Mail-order. Goods posted to you, which you have not in fact ordered, do not have to be paid for nor even posted back at your expense. But keep them intact so that the company concerned can collect them from you.

If you send money for goods which do not arrive, or are unsatisfactory, you can complain to the newspaper which carried the advertisement or to the *Advertising Standards Authority, 1 Bell Yard, London WC2.*

 Medical services. There are tribunals to which you can take your complaint: the local Health Executive can tell you the addresses. In addition, there is an unofficial *Patients' Association, 335 Grays Inn Road, London WC1,* which may help you, and an 'ombudsman' for the Health Service is now being appointed too.

Misdescriptions. Untrue advertisements etc. can be referred to the *Advertising Standards Association, 1 Bell Yard, London WC2.*

Prices. At the time of a price freeze you can refer what you think are illicit price increases to the *Price Commission, Wingate House, Shaftesbury Avenue, London W1.*

Professions. (Lawyers, architects, surveyors, etc.) In many cases, there exists a professional body to which such people are obliged by law to belong (or which they may belong to voluntarily) and which lays down standards of service – and sometimes scales of fees too. If you feel your affairs have been so incompetently handled that you have lost money, or if you believe you have been overcharged, it is worth taking the matter up with the professional organization concerned. Any Citizens' Advice Bureau can tell you where to go.

Rates. There are tribunals to investigate if you feel your home has been too highly rated. Many people are entitled to rate rebates anyway. Enquire at the Town Hall.

Rents. Should you feel you are being overcharged, you can take the matter to the local Rent Officer (enquire at the Town Hall).

Service charges (in flats). There may soon be new legislation under which you will be able to ask for a breakdown of the figures, and challenge them if they seem excessive. Ask the local Citizens' Advice Bureau to advise you.

Service trades (plumbers, builders, hairdressers, laundries, cleaners, electricians, TV repairers, driving schools, removers, travel agents, etc.) You may find the offending trader belongs to an association which will investigate complaints against members and, sometimes, secure compensation for you. They vary in their vigour. Citizens' Advice Bureaux (or the reference section of your public library) may help you locate the association.

Telephone. Similar to gas and electricity.

This Licence

13. The Big Consequences of Small Print

Legal Documents. Leaving your Documents with the Bank. Understanding Legal Language. Reading a Lease. House Insurance Policy. Other Documents.

LEGAL DOCUMENTS

Anyone who gets involved with the sort of transactions discussed in earlier chapters will quickly accumulate a lot of legal documents. They look forbiddingly long (and boring) so most people sign without reading them fully, and promptly forget their existence; perhaps even their whereabouts.

LEAVING YOUR DOCUMENTS WITH THE BANK

So vital are documents like these – insurance policies, HP agreements, leases, share certificates and so forth – that banks will (without charge) look after them for you, locking them up safely in their vaults or safes. You can take them out whenever you want to re-read them. For instance, before making an insurance claim or entering into a dispute with your landlord, it is as well to check just what your rights (or liabilities) are and are not. It is foolish to make a claim to which you are not entitled, or to present it incorrectly.

But, above all, *do read before you sign.* You can argue then about terms you think too harsh, but once you've signed you are committed.

UNDERSTANDING LEGAL LANGUAGE

Legal documents are, for the most part, not difficult to

understand if you take one bit at a time. No harm will be done by using a pencil to underline the most important bits as you go along. *Here are two examples analysed in detail* – a lease and an insurance policy. As you see, almost everything they have to say falls under one of two heads: what benefits and rights are due to you, and what liabilities you have to shoulder.

READING A LEASE

A lease is likely to start off by saying that, in return for what you paid, you have the right to live in the premises concerned. In the case of a flat, it probably also gives you the right to share other parts – perhaps a common entrance-hall, or a garden – and it will guarantee that your pipes etc., shall remain connected to main supplies in the street, that the adjacent structure of the building shall not be pulled down around your ears, and similar essentials. On the other hand, you will have a liability not to tamper with pipes, structure etc., on which others depend, even if they are part of your flat. So far, this is just what you might have taken for granted anyway. But now look out for clauses granting the landlord rights to alter the building, and perhaps to enter into your part in order to do so: how might that affect you in the future?

Expenses. Next might come some clauses about your liability for future payments – what ground rent, rates and service charge are you required to pay? May these go up in later years? What will you be getting for your money? Service charges for flats are a frequent cause of friction: they are theoretically related to what has actually been paid out to keep the building in good shape – something likely to cost more in some years than others, but which goes up as prices generally go up. Under a recent Act of Parliament, tenants are entitled to proper certificates, written by an accountant, explaining what expenses have been met. But many leases purport to give landlords a free hand to name any sum they like. Beware!

Service charges. The lease should state what 'services' you are to receive under this charge: things like cleaning and repair of the common parts, insurance, painting the exterior, upkeep of garden, lighting the stairs, etc. Repairs to 'common parts' will include major things like roof or foundations, even though your flat may not be directly affected by these.

Watch out for clauses that may require you to contribute to 'improvements' you don't in fact want; but do not argue over the inclusion of things which, if neglected, could diminish the value of the property. You should be given the right to verify that the building is fully insured (and that you yourself can make claims under the policy, if need be).

Your responsibilities. A normal liability (but one many tenants forget, when in fact they should be saving up for it) is a requirement to redecorate throughout shortly before moving out – as well as to keep the premises (including plumbing, wiring etc.) in a good state meanwhile. Equally normal is a clause requiring you to leave behind any improvements you've made (built-in cupboards, for example). They become the landlord's property, a point to remember before you lash out on such things. (Plants you put in a garden become his property, too.) The landlord has the right to inspect the interior and, if you fail to get repairs etc. done, to bill you for repairing them himself.

Just how far the latter liability extends could be very important to you. Suppose dry rot occurs: how far will you be liable for what might be the very high cost of eradicating it? It might be not only in floorboards and window frames but in joists and walls too: perhaps the former might be your liability but the latter the landlord's – *does the lease make it clear who pays for what?*

 Restrictions. Another thing to look for is any restriction on the use of the flat or house: there may be clauses preventing you sub-letting, taking lodgers, or carrying on any work there (even if there are not, local town-planning rules may limit what you can do).

If some clauses seem to limit your rights (for instance, prohibitions on making music, keeping pets, leaving floors uncarpeted, allowing children to play in entrance halls or prams to be parked there, shaking mats outside, perching flowerpots on windowsills, playing a radio in the garden, or hanging washing outside), remember that you benefit from the similar restraints placed on people in the adjoining flats. A number of irritations might be avoided if every tenant knew what behaviour his lease expected of him in the first place and acted accordingly.

HOUSE INSURANCE POLICY

Now for a different, and usually simpler, kind of document, an insurance policy. Here are the sort of things you might find in a policy insuring the contents of a house.

Description of premises. The policy is likely to start by describing the premises it insures – stating what the house is made of and what other things are insured (e.g. garage, fences, gates, paths etc.). Immediately, this raises a point to remember: if ever you alter the premises (substituting a flammable thatched roof for a tiled one, for example, or adding a greenhouse) you ought to tell the insurance company.

Disasters covered. Then it will go on to tell you what disasters it covers – though to many of them there will be exceptions, and often you are required to pay the first £10 yourself. A typical policy might cover the effects of such things as these, but with many exceptions:
fire; lightning; thunderbolts; explosion; aircraft crashing on to house; motor (or animals) crashing into house;

theft; malicious damage; riots; strikes; burst pipes, overflows etc.; accidental breakage of glass, sanitary fittings etc.; storms and floods; oil leaks; landslides and subsidence; collapse of TV aerial.

Other points. Major damage may extend beyond the house to pipes connected to the main supplies in the street; it may involve you in renting other premises while your house is repaired; you may have to compensate someone who was injured (or whose property was damaged) through an incident in your house, and to incur legal costs: there should be clauses covering these costs too.

It is obviously well worth reading attentively all these details so that when someone does drop something heavy in a washbasin and cracks it, when a leaky pipe ruins furnishings, or when a gas-cooker explodes, you do not forget to claim the benefit due to you.

OTHER DOCUMENTS

Finally, there are other 'documents' (though you may not think of them as such) which can be as binding in the eyes of the law as any formal contract. Things like estimates and quotations for work or goods; the words in mail-order or other advertisements; bills and receipts; the 'terms and conditions' on the back of booking-forms for holidays, tickets and suchlike. Read them – and keep them. You never know what disagreement or complaint may arise later.

Sale
FUR FELT
HATS
£1·95
Sale
SIZE

14. How Economical Are You?

Food etc. Furniture and Equipment. Repairs and other Services.

FOOD ETC.

Do you often buy the big, economy sizes? Usually but not always the cost per lb is cheaper. But don't buy perishables this way, nor things which might tempt you to consume more. Examples: toothpaste is a good buy in big tubes; but with chocolate you might simply eat twice as much!

Do you regularly buy cheap special offers? When supermarkets offer, say, pineapple at a big saving, it's worth buying several tins. But remember these bargains are meant to tempt you inside, to buy non-bargains too, so be careful! Many supermarkets will often take the '3p off' vouchers that come through the door, even if you don't buy the goods concerned.

Do you plan meals to take advantage of what is in season? Meat, eggs, vegetables and fruit go down in price when there is a glut. Eat pork and cod dishes in winter, for instance; egg dishes in early spring; apples in autumn, pears later. Shoppers late on Saturday often pick up perishables at giveaway prices.

Do you know how to make cheap cuts of meat taste as good as dear ones? You can even roast neck of lamb (for instance) if you do it very slowly and at a very low temperature. Ox cheek makes a tender stew if cooked for at least six hours at the lowest oven setting, or use a pressure-cooker. For good recipes, get S. Atterbury's *Leave It To Cook* (Penguin).

 Do you do any 'bulk buying'? If you have storage space, things like soap, detergent, toilet paper etc. can be bought in big cartons at little more than wholesale prices. Small local shops may give discounts; or look in the local paper for advertisements of 'cash-and-carry' warehouses; use a mail-order supplier like *Buybulk, Tunnel Bank Road, Bourne, Lincolnshire,* or go to the wholesale markets for things like cases of apples or oranges if you eat a lot. Paint, electric flex, etc., are cheaper in bulk.

Do you usually buy unbranded pills, cosmetics etc. at the chemist's? Instead of paying high prices for much-advertised brands of aspirin etc., you can get exactly the same formula without a maker's name on it. Ask the chemist to give you the BP (British Pharmacopoeia) equivalent of whatever it is you need. Similarly, witch hazel, acetone, lanoline, castor-oil-and-zinc, and sodium sesquicarbonate cost a fraction of most skin tonics, nail varnish removers, cold cream, skin cream or bath salts.

Do you make sensible use of the January sales? Many trashy goods are offered then. But among them will be genuine bargains. Things like towels or china marked down merely because of a slight irregularity in the colour are worth having.

Do you buy things loose rather than in packets when you can? Often this means you'll get more for your money – dried vegetables, nails and screws, sweets etc.

Do you compare prices at different shops? Often, chemists are cheaper than grocers for corn oil, spices, vinegar, cornflour etc. and builders' merchants are cheaper than hardware shops for nails, meths etc. Look out for army surplus stores, and bargain basements in department stores.

Do you know which foods give most nutrition for least cost? Liver, cheese, oatmeal, milk, bread, carrots, cabbage, haricot beans, potatoes, spinach, watercress.

Do you use up left-overs? They need not be dull. There are good recipes for them in *Left Over For Tomorrow*, Marika Hanbury Tenison (Penguin, 50p).

FURNITURE AND EQUIPMENT

Do you 'shop around' to discover where you can get the biggest discount for the thing you want? Shops in side streets or suburbs may be cheaper than city-centre ones.

If you're replacing an old appliance, do you ask for a trade-in allowance? Some shops give them, some don't. Alternatives are to sell it through adverts in the local paper or a newsagent's board, or phone a second-hand dealer (addresses in the Yellow Pages of the phone book). Some 'junk' is valuable: old lead pipes, for example.

Do you study comparative reports before you buy? Every month *Which?* publishes the results of tests on a wide variety of goods. Often these show that cheaper makes may be as good as dearer ones. You can get these reports by writing to *Consumers Association, Caxton Hill, Hertford.* (The cost of subscription was uncertain at the time of going to press.)

If you go to shops that accept credit cards, do you ask for a discount if you pay cash? Because on cash purchases the shop does not have to pay a commission to any credit-card company, it can afford to give you maybe 5 per cent off. (Some other organizations, e.g. coal merchants, rates departments, may give discounts for cash.)

Do you belong to or could you join any organization which gets you discounts? Staff clubs, garden or hobby clubs, motoring organizations, trade or professional unions: any of these might save you money, not only on goods but also on services like driving lessons or insurance.

Do you ever buy second-hand? Reconditioned cookers from Electricity and Gas Boards are often a bargain. So are vacuum cleaners and refrigerators if they have had new motors put in. Retread tyres can be a good buy. The wood from old furniture may prove cheaper than new timber. Jumble-sale clothes can provide you with zips etc. for a few pence. Children's clothes, outgrown before being outworn, are worth buying. Some local papers, the weekly *Exchange & Mart* and other periodicals have useful small advertisements of second-hand goods, or of auctions.

Do you use 'screw-it-yourself' kits? These, and whitewood furniture prepared ready to paint, are much cheaper than properly finished furniture. You can usually buy whitewood furniture in large department stores.

REPAIRS AND OTHER SERVICES

Do you always get two or three estimates to compare? For a rewiring job, one firm quoted £176 and another £89; for a TV repair, £10 and £2; for a car repair £10 and £3; for painting a house, £194 and £100. Even laundries, shoe-repairers etc. charge widely different prices, and the dearest is not always the best. Look in the Yellow Pages of your telephone book for addresses.

Do you do any repairs yourself? If you don't know how, why not go to evening classes? (Details are obtainable from your local Education Authority.) Or buy a book like the *Reader's Digest Repair Manual*. The necessary equipment can often be hired (e.g. floor-sanders, trestles, ladders, carpet shampooers, etc.). Some garages provide facilities for do-it-yourself lubrication, repairs etc.

Do you do any other things for yourself? For example, hundreds of pounds can be saved by doing your own house-conveyancing. On this – and on practically anything else you're likely to attempt – there are 'how to' books that make the procedures plain. You can also conduct your own divorce, providing it's without complications. For information on how to do so, see *Women's Rights, A Practical Guide*, Anna Coote and Tess Gill

(Penguin, 60p) or *Breaking Up, a Practical Guide to Separation, Divorce and Coping on your Own,* Rosemary Simon (Arrow, 65p).

Do you take advantage of off-peak discounts? Hairdressers find some days of the week are slack, dry cleaners are idle in certain months, trains run half-empty at certain hours. Many then offer their services cheaply, though they may not publicize this fact unless asked. Pensioners especially may find off-peak facilities going cheap to them – from cinema seats to holidays abroad. In summer, you may get central heating or double glazing done at a discount – also electric blanket servicing, and deliveries of coal or oil.

Before you buy new things, do you think about repairing (or improving) what you've got already? Ask at hardware stores about reconditioning saws, saucepans, oil stoves and wringers; and at electric shops about new motors for refrigerators and vacuum cleaners. Baths can be re-enamelled, shoes refurbished with shoe-paint, pillows and quilts re-made by drycleaners.

Do you know all the money-saving services available to you? Here are some. Water boards which will rewasher taps free. Police Crime Prevention Officers, who will recommend locks that may be cheaper than famous-name ones. Fire stations that will tell you how to fireproof your home economically. And lots of services provided free by local Councils: aids for invalids, records on loan.

When buying new appliances, do you ask about their future repair costs? Unless spares and service are guaranteed to be available, the product may become a write-off prematurely. Cheap clocks, can be unrepairable.

Photographic acknowledgements

J. Allan Cash, 8, 24, 30, 38, 56, 64; Barclays Bank, 20; Romano Cagnoni (Report), 70; Camera Press, 52, 78, 90; Mark Edwards, 44, 60; Robert Enever Associates, 84.

The author wishes to thank Barclays Bank for advice on several chapters of this book.